Take Two

One afternoon,

Grandma went shopping.

She came home with ten bananas.

She put them in a basket

on the kitchen bench.

The next morning,

Dad saw the bananas in the basket.

He was on his way to work.

He took two bananas

and put them in his lunch box.

There were eight bananas left

in the basket.

$$10 - 2 = 8$$

Chris was getting ready for school.

"I like bananas," he said.
"I will have one for my lunch.
And I will take one
for my friend, Luke."

There were six bananas left
in the basket.

$$8 - 2 = 6$$

Emily was getting ready for school, too.

"Bananas are my favourite fruit," she said.

She took two bananas
and put them into her school bag.

There were four bananas left
in the basket.

$$6 - 2 = 4$$

Grandad came inside.

He was very hungry.

He took two bananas
and went outside again.

There were two bananas left
in the basket.

$$4 - 2 = 2$$

Mum came into the kitchen.
"I will make a banana cake,"
she said.

She took the last two bananas.

There were no bananas left
in the basket.

$$2 - 2 = 0$$

At lunchtime,

Grandma came into the kitchen.

"Where did all the bananas go?"
she said.
"There are none left!
The basket is empty."

 $10 - 2 = 8$

 $8 - 2 = 6$

 $6 - 2 = 4$

 $4 - 2 = 2$

 $2 - 2 = 0$